PLANET POLICE

JEWEL
THIEF

Anna Nilsen • Illustrated by Real Time Visualisation

DK PUBLISHING, INC.

Get ready to maze race around the world!

1. Use a pencil to follow the road maze through each city.

2. Drive on the road maze until you come to a yellow circle—this is a **launch pad.**

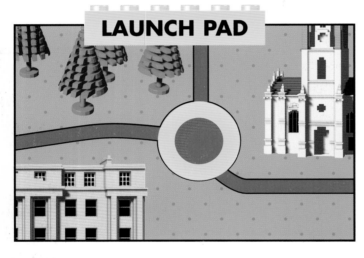

LAUNCH PAD

3. The hole in the center of the launch pad leads to a red **landing pad** on the next set of pages. Whenever you come to a launch pad, you *must* fly through the hole to the landing pad on the next set of pages.

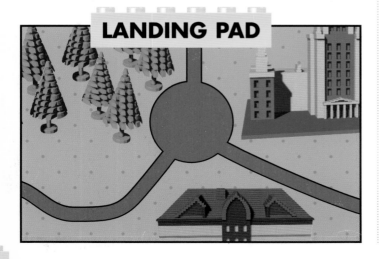

LANDING PAD

TIP: *Don't lose your place!* Before you turn the page, place your pencil eraser on the landing pad and *then* turn the page.

4. On the next set of pages is a new city. Take the maze until you come to another yellow launch pad. Remember—you *must* fly through!

5. If a road is blocked by a car, van, or building, you must turn around and find another route.

BLOCKED ROADS

6. Take a trial run first. See if you can get from Police Headquarters, at the beginning of the book, to City Jail, at the end.

POLICE HEADQUARTERS

Maze Games

Become a crafty criminal in *Crafty Crimes* and *Jail Break*! Or earn your badge as a police officer in *Dawn Raid*.

CRAFTY CRIMES

Be a crafty criminal! Find the route each villain took to get from his or her hideout to the crime scene and back again.

1. Use the Crafty Criminals Crime Board to find each criminal's hideout and crime scene.

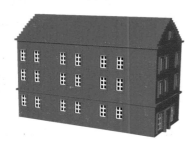

2. First, decide which criminal you want to be, then memorize the name of his or her hideout.

3. Start at your criminal's hideout, then take the maze to the crime scene.

TIP: You can play each criminal in whatever order you like.

Planet Police Warning!
Watch out for the planet police! If they catch you on the road, they'll take you to City Jail, where you *must* start over!

JAIL BREAK

Break out of jail! Find the route each criminal took to break out of jail and reach his or her hideout. Don't get caught by the police!

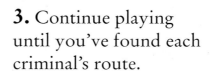

1. Decide which criminal you want to be, then memorize the name of his or her hideout.

2. Start at City Jail, then take the maze to your hideout.

3. Continue playing until you've found each criminal's route.

TIP: You can play each criminal in whatever order you like.

Planet Police Warning!
Watch out for the planet police! They'll take you back to jail, and you'll have to start over!

CITY JAIL

DAWN RAID

Be a Planet Police Officer and make an early-morning raid on those crafty criminals!

Planet Police Warning!
If you come across a police motorcycle on the way, that means another police officer got to the hideout first. Then you *must* go back to Police Headquarters and start over!

MISSION ONE

1. Check out the Crafty Criminals Crime Board to decide which hideout you want to raid. Then memorize the name of the criminal at that hideout.

2. Starting at Police Headquarters, take the road maze to the hideout. Capture the criminal and take the villain to City Jail.

MISSION TWO

Now try to capture *two* criminals in *one* trip!

1. Decide which two hideouts you want to raid.

2. Starting from Police Headquarters, take the maze to the first hideout. Capture the criminal.

3. Continue to follow the maze until you find the second hideout. Capture the second criminal and take *both* villains to City Jail.

Maze Challenge: There are **six** different ways you can catch two criminals—can you find them all?

MISSION THREE

Now try to catch *three* criminals in *one* trip!

1. Decide which three hideouts you want to raid.

2. Starting from Police Headquarters, take the maze to all three hideouts, one after another. Capture the criminals, one by one, and take them to City Jail.

Maze Challenge: There are **three** different ways to catch three criminals—can you find them?

Maze Games

MISSION FOUR
Once you've captured three criminals, you're ready for the ultimate challenge: *all four criminals in one shot!*

. Start from Police Headquarters and take the maze to all four hideouts, one after another. Capture the criminals and take them to City Jail. It's not easy, so good luck!

A s you race around the world, you can see which area of the globe you are in by matching the color of each page border to the color of each landmass on the map below.

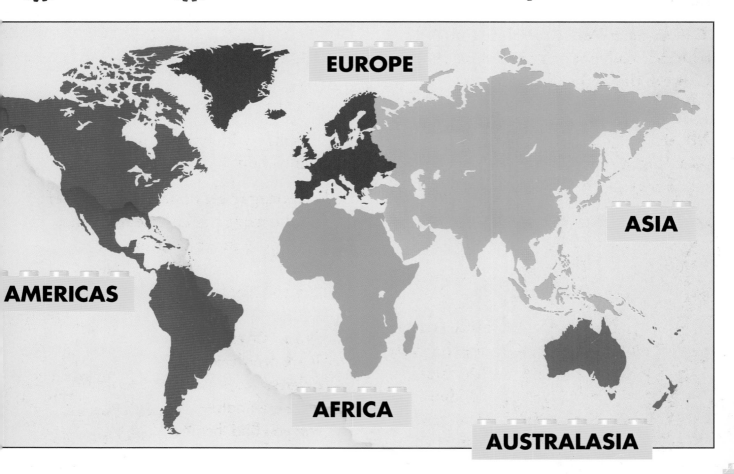

EUROPE

ASIA

AMERICAS

AFRICA

AUSTRALASIA

Planet Police Headquarters

CRAFTY CRIMINALS CRIME BOARD

NAME
Jessie Jameson

CRIME
Stole sack of opals
from factory

CRIME SCENE
Opal factory, Australia

HIDEOUT
New York, U.S.A.

NAME
Hamud Darke

CRIME
Stole priceless
Mozart manuscript

CRIME SCENE
Figarohaus, Austria

HIDEOUT
Tunis, Tunisia

NAME
Helena Theophilus

CRIME
Stole perfume
ingredients list

CRIME SCENE
Scents Perfume Factory,
Tunisia

HIDEOUT
Athens, Greece

NAME
Laslo Kepek

CRIME
Stole ancient
Turkish carpet

CRIME SCENE
Dealer's shop,
Turkey

HIDEOUT
Budapest, Hungary

NEW YORK
U.S.A.

World Financial Center

When it was first built, the Empire State Building was the tallest building in the world

Planet Police ahead!

The Chrysler Building is famous for its silver spire

The Statue of Liberty

The road is blocked – find another route!

The Guggenheim Museum, famous for its modern art

Central Park

The Wharf Theater

The road is blocked – find another route!

SYDNEY
AUSTRALIA

The Victoria Barracks

The Sydney Tower

Sydney Cove

The famous Sydney Opera House

Sydney Hospital

Watch out for the Planet Police!

11

Sail along t
Bosphorus

ISTANBUL
TURKEY

Visit one of
Istanbul's
many
mosques

The Military Academy

Planet Police ahead!

Count the minarets on
the Hagia Sophia

e old city wall is made
of many towers

13

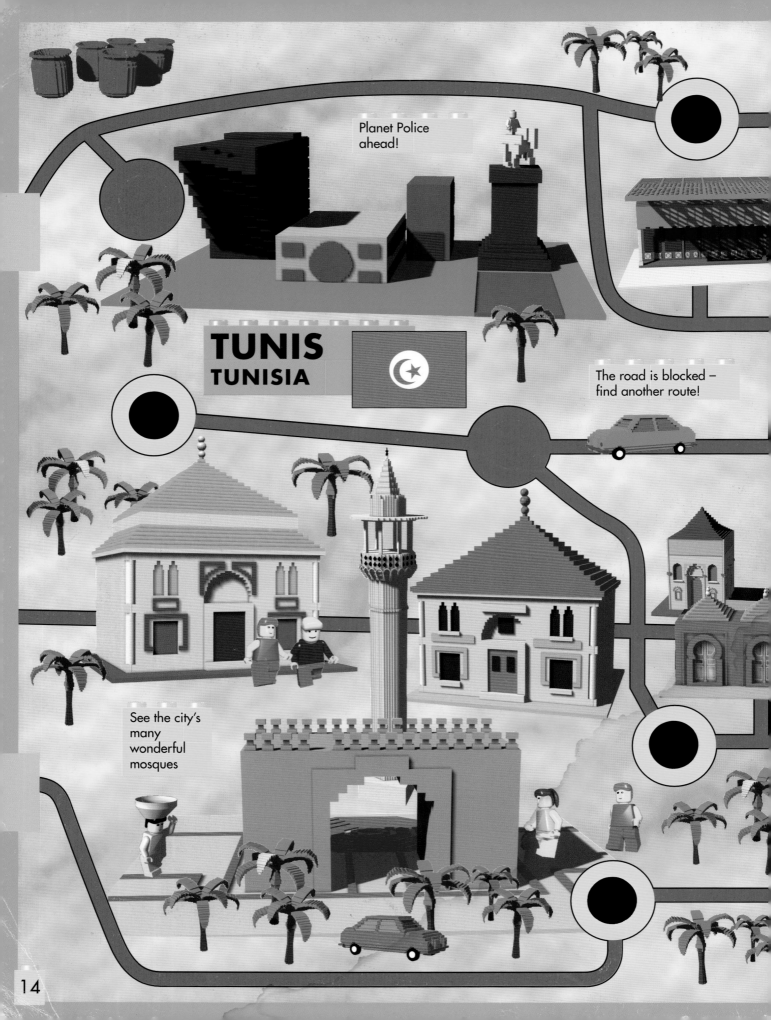

Planet Police ahead!

TUNIS
TUNISIA

The road is blocked – find another route!

See the city's many wonderful mosques

Drill for oil in the Mediterranean

See the Great Mosque from the Palais d'Orient

Look out for the Planet Police!

VIENNA
AUSTRIA

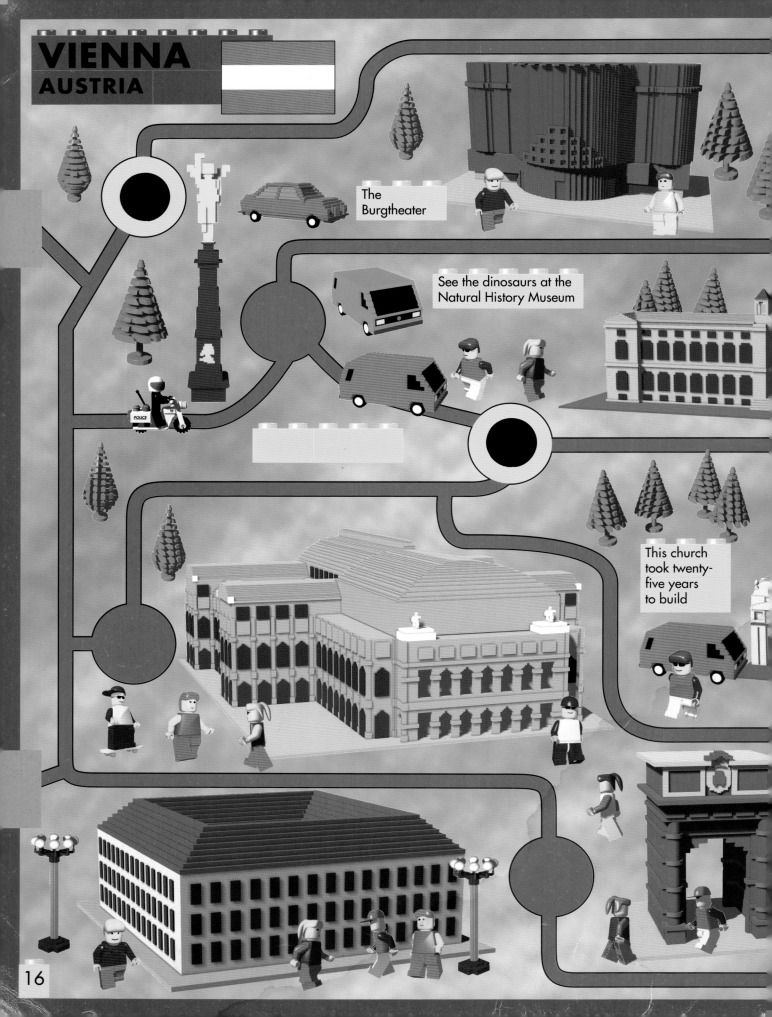

The Burgtheater

See the dinosaurs at the Natural History Museum

This church took twenty-five years to build

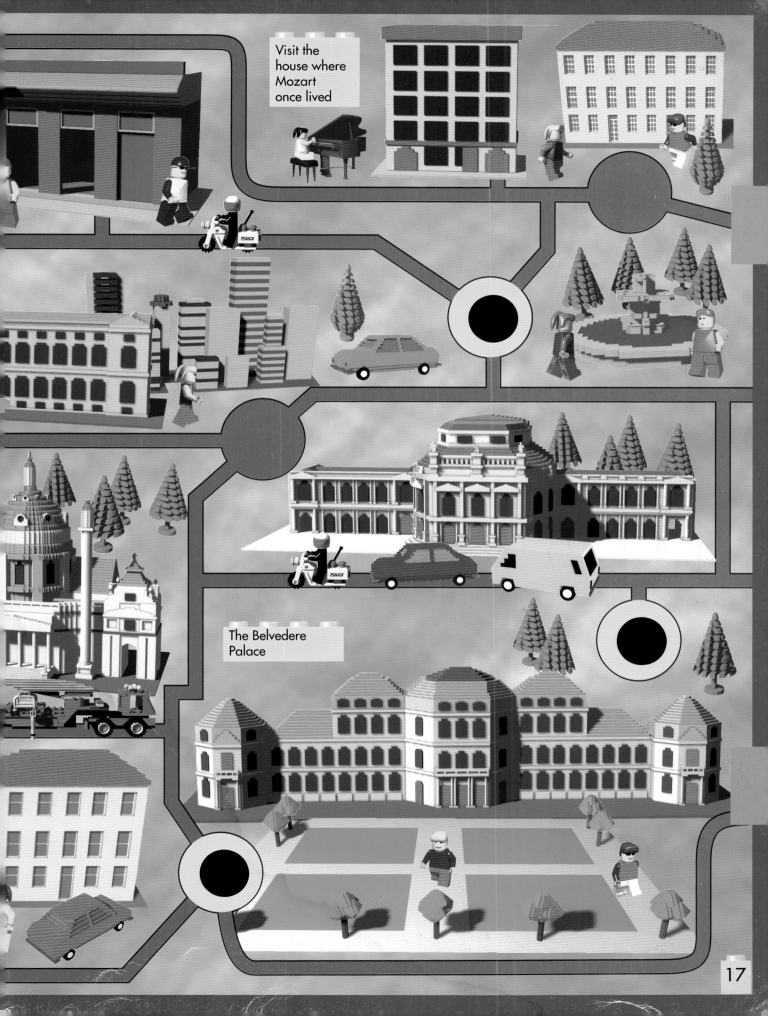

Visit the house where Mozart once lived

The Belvedere Palace

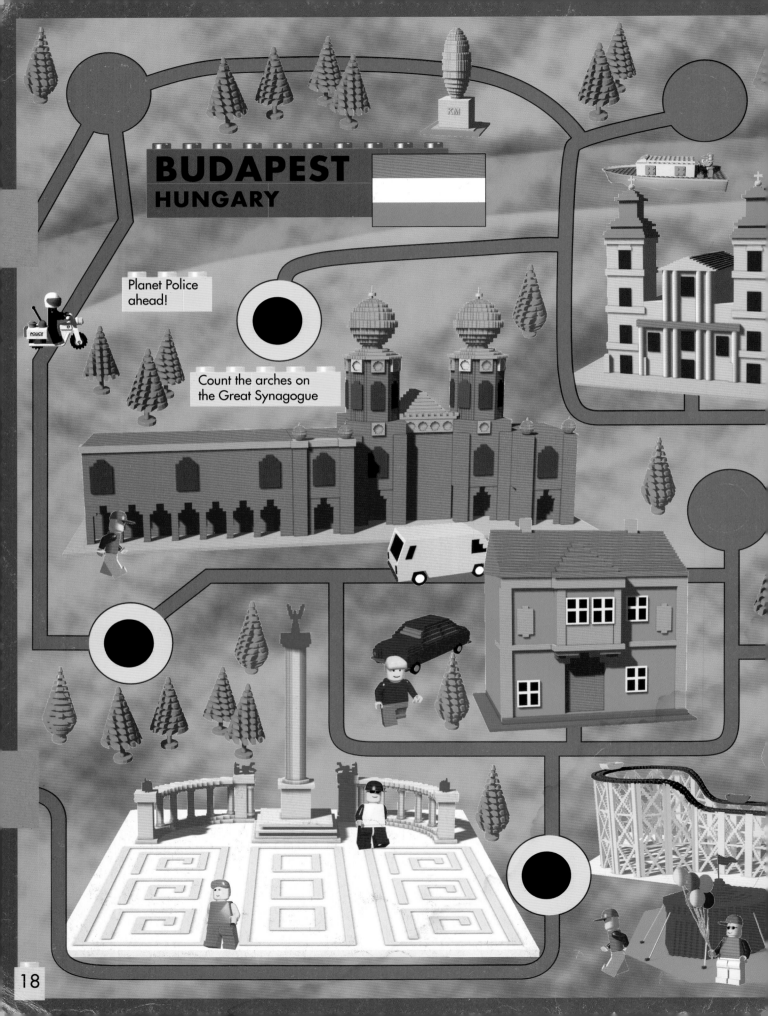

BUDAPEST
HUNGARY

Planet Police ahead!

Count the arches on the Great Synagogue

The government buildings

The city train station

The circus

The city zoo

Climb to the top
of the Acropolis

The old
city stadium

ATHENS
GREECE

Do a tour of the
Byzantine churches

20

Count the pillars
on the Parthenon

The Tower
of Winds

Look out for the
Planet Police!

The flea market

BEIJING
CHINA

Climb the steps of the pagoda

View the Summer Palace from Cixi's Marble Boat

The Gate of Honor

City Jail

Sail under the bridge of Kunming Lake

Watch the stars from the ancient observatory

the Gate of
enly Peace

The Temple of Heaven

Super Maze Games

C ongratulations! You're ready for your next exciting Planet Police book and Super Dawn Raids!

MISSION PREPARATIONS

1. Place two books next to each other so that the border crossings at the side of each page line up. This will let you cross from one book to another.

2. You can only cross to countries on the same mass. These countries will have the same border color. Make sure you cross to a city which has the same border color as the city you are leaving.

JOINING BOOKS

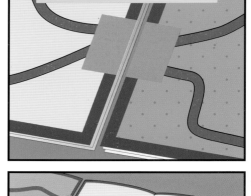

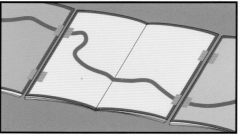

SUPER MISSION ONE

1. Decide from which Police Headquarters you will start your mission and in which City Jail you'll put your criminals.

TIP: You can start from Police Headquarters in one book and put your criminals in City Jail in another.

2. Look at both Crafty Criminals Crime Boards and decide which crafty criminal you are going to catch first.

3. Start by capturing one criminal at a time and then build up to capturing *all eight* on just *one* trip.

SUPER MISSION THREE

1. Finally, place all four Planet Police books next to each other and then try to catch all *sixteen* crafty criminals.

Calling all Planet Police!

Remember – crafty criminals are still at large all over the world. Continue playing to keep crime at bay!

A DK PUBLISHING BOOK

First American Edition, 1998

2 4 6 8 10 9 7 5 3 1

Published in the United States by DK Publishing, Inc.
95 Madison Avenue, New York, New York, 10016.
Visit us on the World Wide Web at http://www.dk.com

Copyright © 1998 Dorling Kindersley Limited, London.

Text copyright © 1998 LEGO Group
Illustrations © 1998 LEGO Group
Devised and written by Anna Nilsen
Illustrated by Real Time Visualisation

ISBN 07894-3653-1

Color reproduction by Flying Colours, Italy
Printed in Hong Kong

SUPER MISSION TWO

1. Now you're ready for your third Planet Police book. Place three books next to each other, in any order you like, and set off to capture all *twelve* villains.